Findings

There are many devices manufactured today that can be used to bridge, connect, and finish beaded and wireworked jewelry. Here are some of them.*

 Lobster clasps, spring rings, and sister clasps can be attached to thread with knots or crimp beads. The clasps lock onto a jump ring attached at the other end of the thread.

 **Hook and eye clasps** are just that—attach the hook to one end of a piece and the eye to the other end. Because the clasp works with gravity, it is good to use with pieces that have some weight (on lighter pieces, the hook and eye tend to travel apart).

 **Crimp beads and tubes** secure loops of unknottable thread such as tigertail. Fold the end of the thread back on itself and slide the crimp bead/tube over and down the doubled thread until you reach a desired loop size. Secure the loop by squeezing the bead/tube tightly with a pliers to "crimp" it to the double-stranded thread. Trim excess thread.

 Knot cups secure and cover knots at the end of a necklace or bracelet. They act as a transition between thread and metal findings. String the cup (domed side first) onto thread and tie several knots. Squeeze the domed sides over the knot, and bend the metal arm down to close cup.

 French earwires or earclips are pierced-earring wire findings with an eye pin attachment for connecting an earring body. Bend the eye pin laterally with a pliers to open, slip on earring body, and bend back to close.

 Jump rings are circles of wire used for connecting findings. To open, bend laterally (rather than make wider).

 End cones cover the ends of beadworked chains, thin loomwork, or thick thread. They act as a transition between the chain body and finding assembly. String thread through end tip and connect finding assembly with knots or crimp beads.

 Brooch backs have a pin assembly and a flat face onto which you can glue or sew a brooch body.

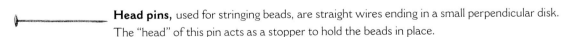 **Head pins,** used for stringing beads, are straight wires ending in a small perpendicular disk. The "head" of this pin acts as a stopper to hold the beads in place.

 **Eye pins** are straight wires ending in a small loop. They are used for stringing beads.

* Excerpted from Beader's Companion, *an essential tool for all beaders from Interweave Press. For more information, see the inside back cover.*

Three Strand Agate Necklace

Keriann Gore

MATERIALS

3' of sinew
1 large etched agate
4 medium cylinder etched agate
14 ostrich shell beads
4 round 4mm carnelian
2 round 8mm carnelian
8 round 6mm carnelian
40 black 4mm glass cubes
3 round 4mm smoky quartz
10 rectangular 4 x 6mm smoky quartz
12 medium fish vertebrae
6 cylinder 8mm fossilized dinosaur bone
240 small terra-cotta African pony beads (size 8° Japanese or Czech beads can be substituted)
2 sterling silver knot covers
Clear nail polish
Bali silver hook and eye

NOTIONS

Awl
Needle-nose pliers
Wire cutters
Scissors

This grand necklace is composed of some very special materials—dinosaur bone, carnelian, smoky quartz, and agate. If it's hard to locate these beads, let the design of the necklace be your guide. Use the approximate bead measurements, colors, and textures to help you find similar beads to create your own special necklace.

Step 1: Split the sinew into three separate lengths. At one end of each length cut so that the sinew is at an angle, then cover about one inch of that end with clear nail polish and let dry completely. At the other end tie all three threads together to make a triple knot that is large enough not to pull through the knot cover. Bring all three threads through the hole of the knot cover, placing the knot inside the cup. Coat the knot with nail polish and pinch the knot cover closed around the knot with pliers.

Step 2: With the three threads together, string the first section (1 black cube, 1 fish vertebrae, 1 dinosaur bone, 1 fish vertebrae, 1 cube). Then split the threads back into three separate pieces and string the second section (First thread: 5 pony beads, 1 rectangle quartz, 3 pony beads. Second thread: 3 pony beads, 1 round quartz, 5 pony beads. Third thread: 4 pony beads, 1 cube, 4 pony beads). Bring the three threads together and string the third section (1 cube, one 6mm carnelian, 1 ostrich shell, 1 agate, 1 ostrich shell, 1 carnelian, 1 cube). See **Figure 1.** Then split the threads and string the fourth section (First thread: 5 pony beads, 1 rectangle quartz, 3 pony beads. Second thread: 3 pony beads, 1 cube, 5 pony beads. Third thread: 3 pony beads, 1 cube, one 4mm carnelian, 1 cube, 3 pony beads).

Repeat in this pattern one and a half more times until you have a total of ten sections.

Figure 1

Step 3: Bring the three threads together and string the center section (1 cube, one 8mm carnelian, 3 ostrich shell, the large agate, 3 ostrich shell, one 8mm carnelian, 1 cube). String the second side as you did in Step 2 but in reverse.

Step 4: To finish your necklace, run the three threads through the back of the knot cover. Make a knot in the thread and, using the awl, bring the knot as far into the knot cover as you can, making it tight against the beads. Before you pull the knot tight, check to see that there are no gaps in the beads. Once the knot is large enough so that it will not pull back through the knot cover, dab clear nail polish on the knot. Use the pliers to pinch the knot cover closed. Cut off any excess thread. Hook the clasp onto the knot cover at the tab, and close the tab with the pliers.

Bead It

Simply Spiraled Earrings

Phyllis Kalionzes

Step 1: Cut 6" of 18-gauge wire.

Step 2: Using a round-nose pliers, start a spiral by creating a loop **Figure 1**. Use a chain-nose pliers to continue spiraling the wire **Figure 2**. Push the wire against the spiral with your thumb as you go to shape it. Stop spiraling when you have a 2" tail **Figure 3**.

Step 3: Flatten the spiral on a bench block with a hammer. Do not flatten the tail.

Step 4: Holding one end of the 24-gauge wire, begin to wrap it around the 18-gauge tail. Continue wrapping close together until you get ½" of coil **Figure 4**. Trim off the ends of the coil and push it in close to the flattened spiral.

Step 5: Holding the spiral with your fingers, finish spiraling the 18-gauge wire **Figure 5**.

Step 6: Use a round-nose pliers to create a back loop for attaching the ear wire **Figure 6**.

Attach the ear wire.

MATERIALS

12" of 18-gauge round silver or gold wire
14" of 24-gauge round silver or gold wire
Silver or gold ear wires

NOTIONS

Wire cutters
Round-nose pliers
Chain-nose pliers
Bench block
Hammer

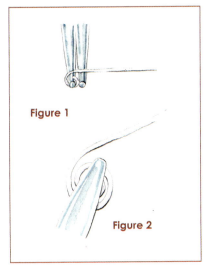

Figure 1

Figure 2

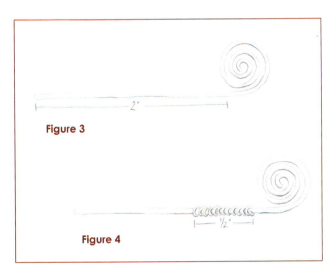

Figure 3

Figure 4

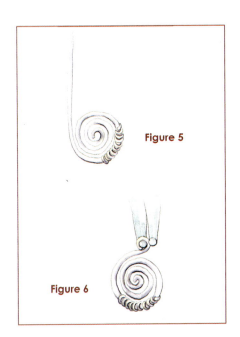

Figure 5

Figure 6

Bead It

Pretty Pearl Pin

Dustin Wedekind

MATERIALS

Six 4mm pearls, crystals, or stones
Size 14° seed beads, in two to three colors
Two 2" squares of stiff felt
Pin back
Size B beading thread

NOTIONS

Size 12 beading needle
Scissors

The ease of bead embroidery allows you to mimic the look of an antique brooch. A few semi-precious stones and an assortment of seed beads offer endless design possibilities. And since the pins work up so fast, you can make one for every color of bead in your stash!

Step 1: Using 3' of thread, pass through the center of the square to the back. Tie a knot in the tail and pass back to the front. String 1 pearl and pass through the felt. Pass back through the pearl a few times to secure.

Step 2: Bring the needle up next to the pearl. *String 4 seed beads and slide them down to the felt. Pass through the felt at the end of the beads. Pass back up slightly behind the second bead. Pass through the last 2 beads again **Figure 1**. Repeat from * to go all around the pearl. On the last stitch, pass through the first bead and into the felt to make a smooth circle of the beads.

Step 3: Repeat Step 2 to make a second ring around the outside of the first ring. Use a solid second color, or alternate the second color with the first color to make a gradation to a third color in Step 5.

Step 4: Work a symmetrical pattern around the pearl. **See chart**. Bring the needle up a bead's width from the outer ring and string a pearl. Pass through the felt and the pearl a few times to secure. Repeat from Step 2. Sew another pearl opposite the last one. Keep going around the central pearl until you can't fit any more pearls (use 6 to 8 pearls).

Step 5: Stitch one or two rows of beads around the entire grouping.

Step 6: Cut the felt 1/16" from the beads all around. Cut the second piece of felt in the same shape. Attach the pin back to the second piece of felt, securing the thread so that it is on the inside of the pin.

Step 7: Holding the two pieces of felt together, exit the thread near the edge of the back piece. Whip stitch the pieces together by *stringing 3 beads and passing through the front piece at the edge of the beads **Figure 2**. Exit the back side a bead's width from the last stitch. Repeat from* to the end. Secure the thread in the felt and trim close to work.

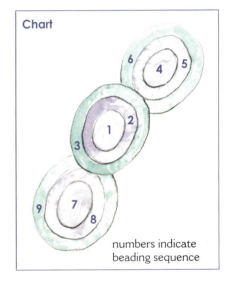

Chart

numbers indicate beading sequence

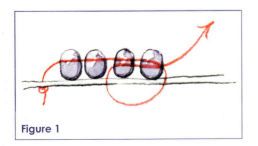

Figure 1

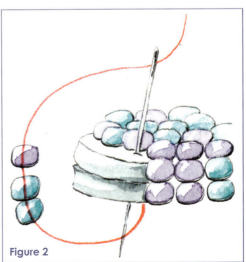

Figure 2

Bead It

The Ribbon Bag

Mary Tafoya

A project that can be completed from start to finish in just a few hours, this ribbon bag is a downright celebration of beads! Use chunky beads and lots of metal findings as you allow the ribbon to dictate a design theme. Keep within a particular cultural style or play with unusual combinations of materials like inexpensive carved bone beside sparkling glass crystals, or turquoise nuggets with vintage faux jet. Hang fringe from the bottom, the flap, and even the strap.

Step 1: Cut a piece of ribbon about 6" long, or longer if the ribbon is wider than 2". Apply sealant to the ends and allow to dry.

Step 2: Cut a piece of interfacing slightly smaller than the ribbon and iron it to the wrong side of the ribbon according to the manufacturer's instructions. Note: Black interfacing is attractive if you can find it, but white is more readily available and provides a place to sign and date the ribbon bag inside the flap.

Step 3: Fold the interfaced ribbon to form a pouch shape. With the wrong side facing up, fold up from the bottom to form the body of the bag, then down from the top to form the flap **Figure 1**. Play with the folds and proportions to create an interesting design. Iron the ribbon to crease the folds. Note: Use low heat for ribbon with metallic threads.

Step 4: Use a crafter's glue stick to temporarily attach the Velcro pieces to the bag. I usually put the hook side on the front of the bag and the loop side under the flap. Using color-coordinated thread, firmly stitch both squares to the ribbon.

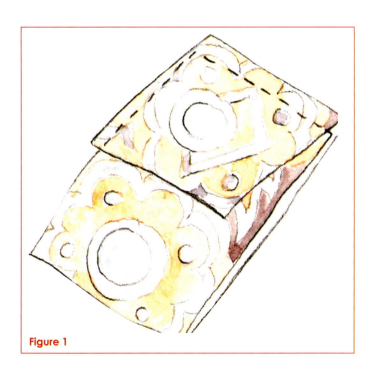

Figure 1

MATERIALS

Size 8° or 11° seed beads

Accent beads for fringe and strap—glass, metal, wood, or bone, in any size or shape

4' of .019" Soft Flex, beading wire

4 to 8 gold or silver crimp beads

Upholstery or beading thread such as Conso, or Silamide

6" of cloth ribbon

Heavy weight white or black fusible interfacing

Fray Check, sealant

Small square of Velcro

Crafters' glue stick

Head pins

Oval jump rings

NOTIONS

Size 10 and 12 beading needles

Crimping pliers

Scissors

Fabric or permanent pen

Iron

Round-nose pliers

Chain-nose pliers

Wire cutters

Ribbon and Closure

Bead Edging

Step 5: Using a yard of thread, tie a knot and leave a 6" tail. Hide the knot by passing the needle down through the bottom layer close to the top edge of the bottom flap (at about 3:00). Take a tiny stitch and come back up through the top layer, close to the edge of the bag **Figure 2**.

Step 6: Working in a clockwise direction, string three beads, go around the edges of the bag, and come up through both layers, about a bead's width from the first stitch. Pass the needle up through the bottom of the third bead and pull snug **Figure 3**. String two beads, go around the ribbon's edge, come up through both layers from the bottom and up through the second of the new beads. The first bead in each pair should stand up vertically, and the second should lie horizontally **Figure 4**. Continue all the way around the bag. Be sure to leave the flap open, sewing the edges together only in the body of the bag.

Step 7: When the circle of edging is almost complete, space the last few stitches to leave room for only one vertical bead in the last stitch. After passing the needle up through the second bead in the last pair, string one bead and pass the needle down through the very first bead in the edging and through the ribbon. Tie the two ends together in a square knot and weave the thread ends through a few edge beads, then trim close to the fabric.

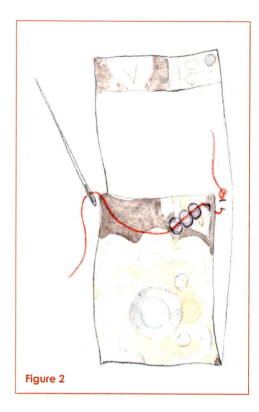

Figure 2

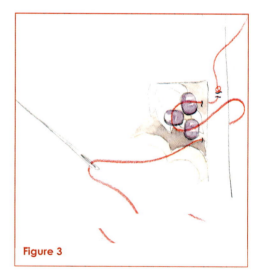

Figure 3

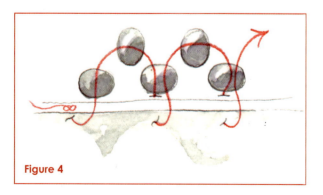

Figure 4

Bead It

Buffer Loops

Step 8: To protect the cloth ribbon from being torn by the Soft Flex wire in the neck strap, attach two loops of beads to the top of the bag, then attach the neck strap to them. First, cut about 1' of thread and tie a knot around a size 11° seed bead. This bead will serve as a "stopper" bead, tucked discreetly under the flap fold. Bring the needle up from under the flap fold, about ¼" in from the edge of the ribbon, and string about 9 seed beads. Note: Always use an uneven number of beads in an attaching loop or the beads will fold in half, exposing the thread and subjecting it to breakage. Pass the needle back down through the flap and through the stopper bead **Figure 5**. Come back up through the ribbon and pass back through the loop of beads. Do this several times, until the bead loop is secure. To secure the thread, pass down through the flap and tie the thread ends in a knot, then bring each end up through three or four loop beads and trim close. Make another buffer loop on the other side of the bag.

Neck Strap

Step 9: Cut a length of wire long enough to slip easily over your head. Add 12". String 1 crimp bead and about 9 seed beads on one end, then bring the end through one of the buffer loops and back through the crimp bead in the opposite direction, to form a loop. Leave about a 3" tail. Secure the crimp bead with the crimping pliers.

NOTE: If the necklace is heavy, I use 2–4 crimp beads on each end of the strap, sometimes separating the crimps with an attractive accent bead.

Step 10: Put several accent beads onto the wire, hiding the tail inside the first several beads. Continue until the strap reaches the desired length. To finish the strap, string a crimp bead and about 9 seed beads, and bring the wire through the second buffer loop and back through the crimp bead in the opposite direction to form a loop. Carefully pull the tail of the wire with the chain-nose pliers until both the strap and the end loop are snug. If possible, push the tail end of the wire into one or more of the accent beads. Flatten the crimp bead and trim the wire end.

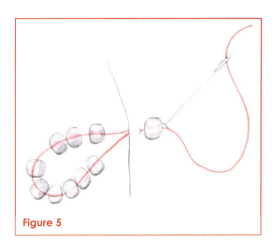

Figure 5

Fringe

Step 11: Cut two yards of thread, double, and tie a knot in the end, leaving a 1" tail. Bury the tail by passing the needle inside the ribbon bag and coming out through the bottom fold near the left or right side of the bag. Bring the needle through the first two beads in the edging (one horizontal and one vertical bead). String any combination of seed and accent beads. Skip the last bead you strung and pass back through all the beads, exiting at the first fringe bead. Pass back through the vertical bead in the opposite direction, up through the next horizontal bead, and take a stitch in the ribbon before passing back through the same horizontal bead. Work the needle through the edging beads, taking stitches into the ribbon as necessary, and come out at a horizontal edging bead to hang the next strand of fringe. Continue this process across the bottom of the bag. To secure the last strand of fringe, take a stitch into the ribbon and tie a secure knot. Then bring the needle through a few edging beads on the side of the ribbon and tie a few more knots. Pull the needle through the ribbon and into the inside of the bag, pull the thread tight, and carefully trim the end.

Charms

Step 12: Hang charms and headpin dangles from jump rings attached to loops of beads in the fringe. These additions create a more durable fringe with lots of interest and movement.

Golden Caterpillar

Jean Campbell

This shiny yet fuzzy creature is deceptively simple to make. A series of picots between Swarovski crystals is all it takes. Extra passes between the crystals means a fuzzier bracelet.

Step 1: Using a yard of thread and leaving a 6" tail, string 1 crystal, the clasp bead, 1 crystal, and 3 seed beads. Skipping the seed beads, pass back through the last crystal strung, the clasp bead, and the next crystal. Tie a square knot **Figure 1**.

Step 2: String 3 seed beads and 1 crystal. Repeat this sequence for the circumference of your wrist. Finish with 3 seed beads.

Step 3: String enough seed beads to create a loop that fits tightly around the clasp bead. Pass back through the last 3 seed beads and the last crystal strung in Step 2 **Figure 2**.

Step 4: String 6 seed beads. Skipping the last three beads strung, pass back through the third bead strung. String 2 seed beads and pass through the next crystal **Figure 3**. Continue across, creating these picots between crystals.

Step 5: To turn the thread around, simply weave through the clasp bead and three seed beads at the end. Continue back across to make more picots. Once you've reached the loop end, weave your thread through those beads to turn your thread around.

Make at least five sets of picots. To create a fuller look, make more picots. End working and tail threads by weaving them through several beads to secure. Tie square knots between beads and pull the thread through several more beads to hide the knots. Trim close to work.

MATERIALS

Size 11° seed beads
10–15 Swarovski 6mm bicone crystals
18mm clasp bead
Size D beading thread in color to match seed beads

NOTIONS

Size 12 sharps or beading needles
Scissors

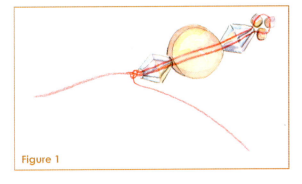

Figure 1

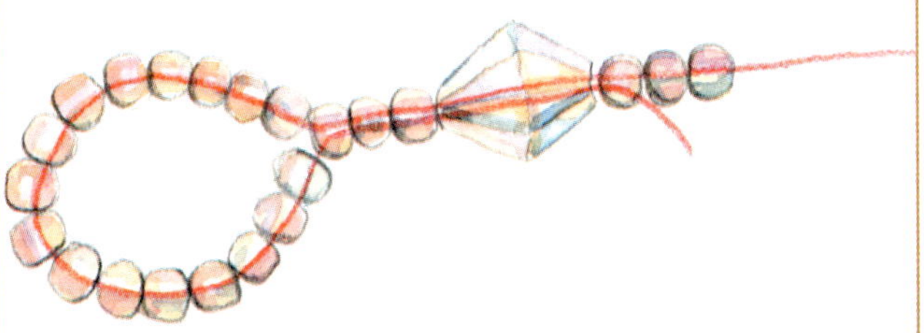

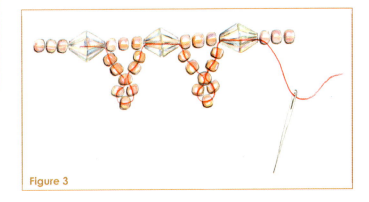

Figure 2

Figure 3

Bead It

Tibetan Power Bead Necklace

Phyllis Kalionzes

This silver and stone necklace is made with materials deemed precious in old Tibet. Turquoise was much revered as warding off the evil eye, and coral was worn only by the wealthiest nobility. Made with simple wireworking techniques, you'll be able to make this power bead necklace with ease.

Long Links

Make 10.

Step 1: Without cutting the wire, and leaving a 1½" tail, use a round-nose pliers to make a single wrapped loop. Wrap the tail wire twice down the working wire to make a hangman's noose loop.

NOTE: Mark a line around your pliers with a permanent marker to keep your loops the same size.

Step 2: Measure 1" from the end of the wrap and bend a 90° angle. Make a two-wrap hangman's noose loop at the bend.

Long Wrapped links

Make five (use five of the ten long links you made above).

Step 3: Holding the 24-gauge wire against the loop, begin wrapping one of the links created in Step 2 **Figure 1**. Wrap tightly, coiling right next to previous coil. Coil as close as you can to end, then trim off uncoiled wire at the beginning. Push the coil as far as possible to beginning and finish wrapping several more wraps to end. Trim.

Turquoise Links

Make five.

Step 4: String a turquoise bead on 18-gauge wire. Make a three-wrap hangman's noose loop. Use a chain-nose pliers to make a 90° angle bend at the same distance you used for the top loop (about ⅛") and a round-nose pliers to finish the three-wrap hangman's noose. Keep these loops the same size as the long wrapped link.

Coral Links

Make five.

Step 5: Make the same as the turquoise links, but thread on a Bali bead cap on each side of the coral.

Assembling the Necklace

Step 6: Open 1 jump ring **Figure 2** and thread on 1 long link and 1 turquoise link. Close the jump ring. Open another jump ring and thread through the same two links alongside the previous jump ring. Repeat. You will have three jump rings connecting the links.

Continue connecting in the following pattern:
Coral link
Wrapped long link
Turquoise link
Long link
Continue until you return to the first link.

Step 7: Oxidize with a liver of sulfur solution. Buff with #0000 fine steel wool and polish with Sunshine Cloth.

MATERIALS

12' of 18-gauge silver wire
50" of 26-gauge silver wire
10 Bali silver bead caps
5 turquoise 15–18mm beads
5 coral 7–8mm beads
Sixty 18-gauge jump rings

NOTIONS

Wire cutters
Round-nose pliers
Chain-nose pliers
Liver of sulfur solution
#0000 fine steel wool
Sunshine Cloth

Figure 1

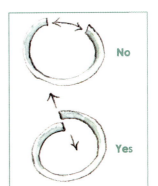

Figure 2

Bead It

Pennington's Kilty Brooch

Jean Campbell

This simple project yields dramatic results. Different pin finishes, chain colors, and bead types will alter the look.

MATERIALS
1" cylinder lampworked bead
2 size 6° seed beads
Three-looped 3" kilt pin
Silver head pin
5" silver chain

NOTIONS
Flat-nose pliers
Round-nose pliers
Wire cutters

Lampworked bead created by Marilynn Dondero-Rich.

Step 1: String 1 seed bead, the lampworked bead, and 1 seed bead on the head pin.

Step 2: At ¼" from the last seed bead strung, make a 90° angle bend with the flat-nose pliers to create a "neck" **Figure 1**.

Step 3: Using the round-nose pliers, bend the wire right at the 90° angle to make a half-loop **Figure 2**. Weave the end of the head pin through the middle loop of the kilt pin.

Step 4: Bend the end of the head pin down and around the neck of the head pin.

Step 5: Grasp the loop you just created with the flat-nose pliers. With the round-nose pliers, grasp the end of the head-pin wire and tightly wrap the neck of the wire down to the seed bead **Figure 3**.

Step 6: Use the wire cutters to trim any excess wire. Push the wire end in line with the wrap by gently squeezing it with the flat-nose pliers.

Step 7: Use the wire cutters to make cuts in the end of the chain so that the last links turn into jump rings. Attach one end to the first loop of the kilt pin, the other end to the third loop.

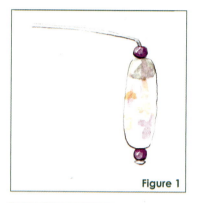

Figure 1

Figure 2

Figure 3

Cirque de Lazuli Earrings

Jean Campbell

MATERIALS
2 silver head pins
Two ½" Bali silver cones
2 Bali silver daisy spacers
2 lapis lazuli 11mm beads
2 silver ear wires

NOTIONS
Wire cutters
Round-nose pliers
Flat-nose pliers

This unusual combination of silver cones and lapis lazuli beads makes a great pair of earrings that will instantly become your favorites.

Step 1: String 1 silver spacer, 1 lapis lazuli, and 1 cone on a head pin.

Step 2: Cut the head pin about ½" from the top of the cone.

Step 3: Using the round-nose pliers, grasp the end of the head pin and slowly wrap the end of the wire twice around the end of the pliers.

Step 4: Attach the ear wire by gently opening the ear wire loop with your flat-nose pliers. Open the ear wire so that the circumference of the loop stays the same—do not widen the loop or the wire will become brittle and break.

Step 5: Repeat all steps for second earring.

Ruby Red Sunset Necklace

Marilyn Koponen

Make this garnet and gold-tone necklace for a festive night on the town. Perfect for a formal function or simple enough for a casual dinner. Let the crystal sparkle, gold shimmer, and beauty of lampworked beads be the highlight of the evening!

Lampworked beads created by Lauri Copeland/Wildfire Designs

Step 1: Measure the length you'd like your necklace to be. Use this measurement plus 5" and cut three even lengths of bead wire.

Step 2: To form the pattern on the end of the necklace, put a clip on one end of the first strand and string four size 8°s and eight size 11°s. Put a clip on the second strand and string eight size 11°s and four size 8°s. Put a clip on the third strand and string four size 8°s, four size 11°s, and four size 8°s.

Step 3: String the 7mm crystal, the 14mm lampworked bead, and another 7mm crystal bead on all three strands at once.

Step 4: Separate the strands and string two size 8°s, four size 11°s, and one oval crystal bead on the first strand. String four size 11°s, two size 8°s, and four size 11°s on the second strand. On the third strand string one oval crystal bead, four size 11°s, and two size 8°s.

Step 5: Repeat Step 3.

Step 6: Repeat Step 4 but twist the strands tightly so that the beads alternate and stand out. Twisting will add color and texture to the necklace.

Step 7: Repeat Step 3.

Step 8: Repeat Step 4.

Step 9: String the 7mm crystal bead, the 20mm lampworked bead, and another 7mm crystal bead on all strands at once.

Step 10: Repeat Steps 4 and Step 3 in that order until all of the 14mm lampworked beads have been used.

Step 11: Repeat Step 2 without using the clips.

Step 12: Separate the strands. Take the first strand, put on a crimp bead, feed it through the eye pin and back through the crimp bead. Crimp.

Repeat for the other two strands. Trim off the excess wire.

Pull the eye pin (straight wire side) through the cone. Cut to ½" outside the cone. Attach a jump ring to the straight end. Using the round-nose pliers, make a loop and capture the jump ring within the loop **Figure 1**.

Step 13: Repeat to complete the other end of necklace. Attach a clasp to the jump rings at each end of the necklace.

MATERIALS

One 20mm lampworked bead
Six 14mm lampworked beads
Fourteen 7mm garnet faceted crystal beads
Twelve 7 x 5 topaz faceted oval crystal beads
Size 11° cream seed beads
Size 8° yellow topaz matte seed beads
Two gold cones
Two gold eye pins
Six gold crimp beads
Two gold jump rings
Gold clasp
Size .18" gold Beadalon wire

NOTIONS

3 clips
Crimping pliers
Round-nose pliers
Wire cutters

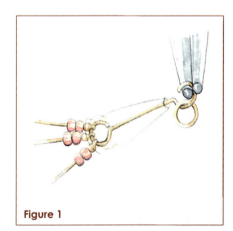

Figure 1

Papyrus Earrings

Linda Gettings

These Egyptian-style earrings are made with brick stitch, a weave common in Cleopatra's era. They look complicated, but the large beads make weaving them a snap.

Step 1: Using 1 yard of thread and a 6" tail, create a foundation row of dark blue hexes in ladder stitch 7 beads long **Figure 1**.

Step 2: Exiting from the top of the first bead in your foundation row, string 2 dark blue hexes and catch the second exposed loop on top of the foundation row **Figure 2**. Pass back through the second bead strung. Continue across the row, stringing one hex, catching the next exposed loop, and passing back through the bead to the end of the row.

Step 3: When you come to the end of the row, work your way across the other way, using the exposed loops you created in the row from Step 2. You will automatically create a decrease each row. Continue creating rows until you are left with only a two-bead row.

Step 4: String 1 size 14°, 1 gold flower, 1 size 14°, and 1 ear wire. Pass back through the size 14° just strung and the flower. String 1 size 14° and pass back through the dark blue hex. Loop through these beads and the ear wire three or four times to secure. Weave back down through the work and exit from the first bead in the foundation row going down.

Step 5: Work this middle section of the earring as you did for Steps 2 and 3 except, in the second row, change your hexes to light blue. The third row will change the second and third beads to light blue and the fourth row uses light blue for all the beads.

Step 6: The fifth row employs increasing. Instead of catching the second loop after you have strung your first two beads, you catch the first loop. This will cause your first bead to pop out over the first bead in the row below. Continue across the row, stringing one bead and catching the next loop.

When you reach the end of the row, you will need to add one last bead without an available loop. Simply string a bead and secure it to the last bead added by weaving it to the side of the second-to-last bead. Weave into the last 2 beads at least 2 times, going down through the last bead in the previous row and figure-8 yourself back around and out the top of the last bead you added **Figure 3**. Do the same thing for the sixth row, using all light blue beads from now on.

Step 7: Rows 7, 8, and 9 are done in all light blue decreasing brick stitch as in Steps 2 and 3.

Step 8: Exit from one of the last hexes added. String 1 size 14°, one 3mm, 1 size 14°, 1 flower bead, 1 size 14°, one leaf, and 1 size 14°. Skipping the last size 14° strung, pass back through all the beads just added and pull the slack in the thread. Pass through the hex and into the adjoining hex. Create another fringe leg. Continue up the side of the diamond. When you have finished with one side, weave your thread to the other side of the diamond and make fringe legs there.

Weave both tail and working threads through several beads to secure. Tie a square knot between beads and pull thread through beads to hide the knot. Trim close to work.

MATERIALS

Dark blue hex or twisted hex beads
Light blue hex or twisted hex beads
Nine 11mm leaf beads
10 gold 3–4mm flower beads
9 blue 3mm round faceted beads
Size 14° blue irid seed beads
Size A or B beading thread in color to blend
2 gold ear wires

NOTIONS

Size 10 Japanese needles
Scissors

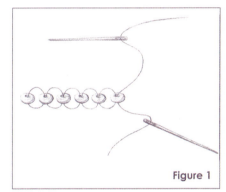

Figure 1

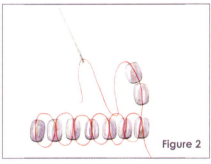

Figure 2

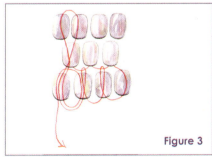

Figure 3

Classic Neutrals

Keriann Gore

This lovely necklace works well for work or casual wear, and it's a perfect way to show off some of your favorite lampworked treasures. The basic design foundation is provided—now feel free to experiment with bead colors, textures, and finishes to make the necklace your own!

Pendant

Step 1: String 1 triangle spacer, 1 lampworked bead, 1 spacer, 1 ostrich shell, 1 spacer, 1 lampworked bead, and 1 triangle spacer on the head pin. Use the needle-nose pliers to bend a right angle about 1/8" above the beads to create a neck **Figure 1**. Using the round-nose pliers, grip the wire about 1/4" from the angle and roll up and over toward the angle, forming a full circle **Figure 2**. Wrap the remaining wire around the neck until the wire meets with the beads **Figure 3**. Cut off any excess wire.

Necklace

Step 2: Using 2' of wire, tape down one end to keep beads from falling off as you string them.

Step 3: String 1 silver bead, one 8mm green glass, 3 ostrich shell, 1 Bali spacer, 3 ostrich shell, one 8mm green glass, 1 silver bead, one 8mm green glass, 3 ostrich shell, 1 Bali spacer, 3 ostrich shell, one 8mm green glass, 1 silver bead, one 6mm green glass, 1 fish vertebrae, 1 tan/green 3-slice, 1 fish vertebrae, one 6mm green glass, 1 silver bead, one 8mm green glass, 3 ostrich shell, 1 Bali spacer, 3 ostrich shell, one 8mm green glass, 1 transparent 3-slice, 1 fish vertebrae, 1 silver bead, one 8mm green glass, 3 ostrich shell, 1 Bali spacer, 3 ostrich shell, one 8mm green glass, 1 small spacer, 1 silver cylinder, 1 small spacer, 1 fish vertebrae, 1 tan/green 3-slice, 1 fish vertebrae, one 6mm green glass, and the pendant.

Step 4: Repeat Step 3 in reverse to string the other side of the necklace.

Step 5: String one crimp bead on the wire and pass through the loop of your clasp. Pass back through the crimp bead to form a loop in the wire. Note: You don't want to remove the gap between the clasp and the beads, because it will be removed when you finish the other side. Snug the crimp bead up to the clasp, then crush it with the needle-nose pliers. Slide all the beads toward the end you have just completed, running the tail of the wire through a few of the beads if the hole size permits. Snip off excess wire.

Step 6: On the opposite end of the wire, remove tape, string on one crimp bead, pass through the loop of the other end of the clasp, go back through your crimp bead, and snug the crimp against the clasp, removing any gaps in the beads before crimping. Crimp with the needle-nose pliers, and snip off any excess wire.

MATERIALS

2 small lampworked beads
2 small Bali beaded spacers
49 ostrich shell beads
10 large Bali silver beaded triangle spacers
16 green 8mm glass beads
4 opaque tan/green 8mm 3-slice glass beads
2 transparent brown 8mm 3-slice glass beads
12 medium fish vertebrae beads
14 different medium-sized Bali silver beads
6 green 6mm glass beads
1 Bali silver balled head pin
1 medium to large Bali silver ring and bar
Two 2 x 3 sterling silver crimp beads
2 feet of .014" Soft Flex wire

NOTIONS

Needle-nose pliers
Round-nose pliers
Wire cutters
Tape

Figure 1

Figure 2

Figure 3

Bead It

Bead It

Wacky Wrap Pearl Earrings

Phyllis Kalionzes

Step 1: Cut 20" of 24-gauge wire.

Step 2: Leaving a 4" tail, make a double loop by going around the round-nose pliers twice **Figure 1**. String 3 pearls onto the working wire.

Step 3: Wrap the tail wire down the working wire 5 or 6 times to measure $\frac{1}{8}$". Push the first pearl up to meet the coil just made **Figure 2**. Wrap the tail down over that pearl and coil down about three times **Figure 3**.

Step 4: Push up the next pearl, wrap the tail down over the pearl, and coil 3 times. Trim off tail.

Step 5: Push up the last pearl to meet the coil. Use the working wire to wrap up over the last pearl and loosely coil up between the last and the second pearl 7 or 8 times.

Step 6: Wrap up over the second pearl (on the opposite side that you wrapped down) and loosely wrap around that coil 7 or 8 times **Figure 4**.

Step 7: Wrap up over the top pearl and loosely wrap 7 or 8 times, ending close to the pearl. Cut and hide end in wraps **Figure 5**.

Step 8: Attach ear wire. Oxidize if you wish with a solution of liver of sulfur, buff with fine steel wool, and polish with a Sunshine Cloth.

MATERIALS

6 freshwater pearls

40" of 24-gauge round silver or gold wire

Ear wires

NOTIONS

Wire cutters

Round-nose pliers

Liver of sulfur solution

#0000 fine steel wool

Sunshine Cloth

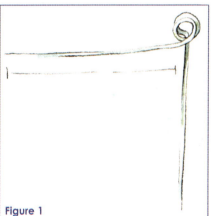
Figure 1

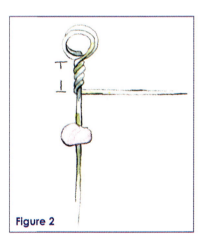
Figure 2

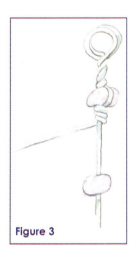
Figure 3

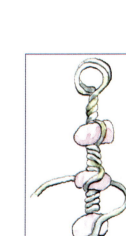
Figure 4

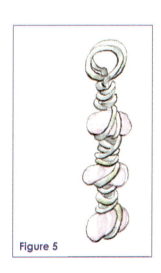
Figure 5

Bead It

Them Bones Bracelet

Jean Campbell

> This multi-layered bracelet is reminiscent of 1950s pearl bracelets, but you make it of bone! You can purchase a reasonably-priced mixed bag of bone beads from several mail-order bead houses or from your local bead shop.

MATERIALS

Approximately 125 white bone beads, 6mm–11mm

4 horn 1⅜" four-holed spacers

Memory wire

NOTIONS

Flat-nose pliers

Step 1: Measure 1½ coils of memory wire and bend the wire at this measurement back and forth until it snaps. Repeat so you have four coils. Note: Do not attempt to cut this kind of wire with a cutters because it will mar your blade.

Step 2: Use your flat-nose pliers to make a small bend at one end of the wire. Pinch hard enough so that the wire end touches the body of the wire **Figure 1**.

Step 3: String 1 small bead and the spacer on the top rung. Next, string nearly ⅓ of the wire with beads. String another spacer at the top rung. String nearly ⅓ of the wire with beads. String another spacer at the top rung. String almost the rest of the wire with beads, finish with a spacer at the top rung and a small bead. Cinch up the beads on the wire and bend the wire end back on itself to secure the beads **Figure 2**. If you have extra wire, choose the place you'd like to end it and bend it back and forth until the wire snaps.

Step 4: Repeat Steps 2 and 3, using the spacers that are already in place. Work your way down the spacers' rungs, next coiling your way through rung 2, then rung 3, and finally rung 4. Be conscious of bead position and how it affects the beads placed in the rungs above.

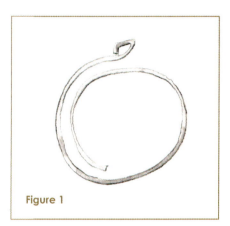

Figure 1

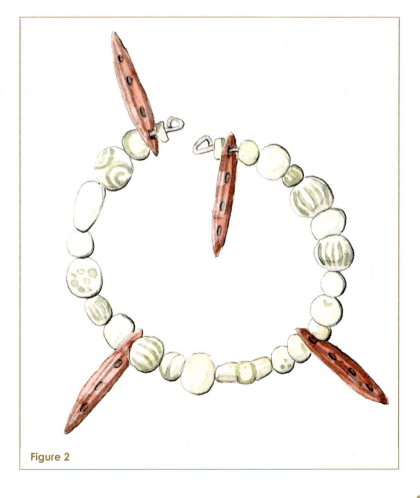

Figure 2

Elegant Silvers

Keriann Gore

This striking necklace is made with smoky quartz faceted beads and is highlighted by Bali silver. If you can't find these exact beads, explore at the bead store—stretch your imagination and use beads with similar shapes.

Step 1: Using 2' of wire, tape down one end to keep beads from falling off as you string them **Figure 1**.

Step 2: String 1 rondelle, 1 spool, 1 rondelle, 3 heshi, 1 rondelle, 1 spool, 1 rondelle, 3 heshi, 1 rondelle, 1 spool, 1 rondelle, 3 heshi, 1 rondelle, 1 spool, 1 rondelle, 3 heshi, 1 rondelle, 1 spool, 1 rondelle, 1 triangular spacer, 1 smoky quartz, 1 triangular spacer, 1 rondelle, 1 silver round, 1 rondelle, 1 square spacer, 1 smoky quartz, 1 square spacer, 1 rondelle, 1 silver round, 1 rondelle, 1 triangular spacer, 1 smoky quartz, 1 triangular spacer, 1 rondelle, 1 silver round, 1 rondelle, 1 square spacer, 1 smoky quartz, 1 square spacer, 1 rondelle, and 1 large cylinder.

Step 3: Repeat Step 3 in reverse to string the other side of the necklace.

Step 4: String one crimp bead on the wire and pass through the loop of your clasp. Pass back through the crimp bead to form a loop in the wire **Figure 2**. Note: You don't want to remove the gap between the clasp and the beads, because it will be removed when you finish the other side. Snug the crimp bead up to the clasp, then crush it with the needle-nose pliers. Slide all the beads toward the end you have just completed, running the tail of the wire through a few of the beads if the hole size permits **Figure 3**. Snip off excess wire.

Step 5: On the opposite end of the wire, remove tape, string on one crimp bead, pass through the loop of the other end of the clasp, go back through your crimp bead, and snug the crimp against the clasp, removing any gaps in the beads before crimping. Crimp with the needle-nose pliers, and snip off any excess wire.

MATERIALS

34 faceted black 4mm–6mm rondelles
1 large Bali silver cylinder
8 faceted cylindrical 8mm x 16mm smoky quartz
10 Bali silver spools
6 medium-sized Bali silver rounds
24 Bali silver beaded heshi
8 medium-sized Bali silver flat squares
8 large Bali silver beaded triangular spacers
1 Bali silver S-hook with rings
Two 2 x 3 sterling-silver crimp tubes
2 feet of .014" Soft Flex wire

NOTIONS

Needle-nose pliers
Tape
Wire cutters

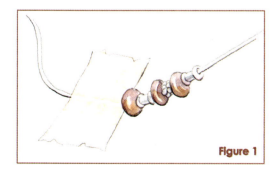

Figure 1

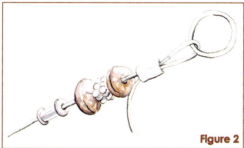

Figure 2

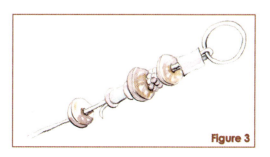

Figure 3

Bead It

Chart

Bead It

Floral Fantasy Bracelet

Sharon Bateman

This pretty little bracelet is a great sampler for learning how to follow a bead chart and do basic flat peyote stitch and decreasing. And the blossoms bring springtime to any day of the year!

Step 1: Using 2 yards of thread and following the chart, string the first bead. Slide it down to 18" from the end of the thread. Pass through the bead again **Figure 1**.

Step 2: String 1 black, 3 red, 3 blue, and 5 white.

Step 3: Begin to work peyote stitch by creating a third row (the first beads you strung will create the first and second rows), following the color placement in the chart. To work this row, string a bead and pass through the second-from-the-last bead strung in

Step 2: **Figure 2**. String 1 bead. Skip a bead and pass through the next bead from the beads strung in Step 2. Continue across, stringing a bead, skipping a bead, and passing through a bead until you reach the end of the row. As you work each row of peyote, the last row of beads will stand up from the end of your work. These will be called stand-up beads.

Step 4: When you get to the end of the row, make a U-turn and begin the next row in the opposite direction. Continue to follow the chart, stringing on the next bead and passing through the next stand-up bead. Add subsequent rows as you follow the chart.

Step 5: At the end of the pattern, decrease at the end of the rows. This decrease will form a point so you can add a clasp. To decrease simply make your U-turn on the second stand-up bead in from the last bead **Figure 3**.

Weave your thread through the beads, bringing it to the inside of the last two stand-up beads.

Step 6: Add a clasp by stringing on 2 black beads, the clasp bead, and 1 black bead. Skip the last black bead and pass back through the clasp bead and the first 2 beads. Pass through the green stand-up bead and pull everything tight. Run through the beads back to the black stand-up bead. Pass through all again twice to strengthen.

Step 7: Finish the other side by using the 18" of tail thread you left hanging. Thread your needle with this thread and work the second point. Follow the chart for color placement. Once you have made the second point, weave through the beads until your thread exits from the inside of one of the stand-up beads.

Step 8: Add a clasp loop by stringing 26 beads. Pass back through the first two strung. Pass through the second stand-up bead of the point and pull everything tight **Figure 4**. Pass back through the beads of this point and through the loop beads two more times for strength.

MATERIALS

2-gram packs of Magnifica beads in white, green, black, red, yellow, blue, purple, and pink

1 faceted 10 x 8mm glass clasp bead (Mill Hill Glass Treasure 12251)

Silamide thread

NOTIONS

Size 12 beading needle

Scissors

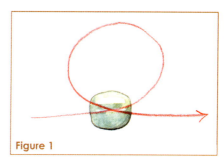

Figure 1

Figure 2

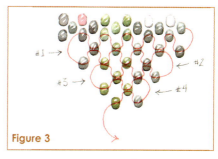

Figure 3

Figure 4

Loop-De-Loop Earrings

Barbara L. Grainger

These easy earrings can be made in an evening. Change seed bead color and focal bead size and color for a variety of looks.

Step 1: Using about a yard of thread, and leaving a 6" tail, string 4 size 11° seed beads and tie a knot to make a circle **Figure 1**.

Step 2: String one 8mm focal bead and 50 seed beads. Pass back through the focal bead to make a looped fringe **Figure 2**.

Step 3: *Pass the needle through all four of the top circle of beads, and back through the focal bead. String 50 seed beads and pass back through the focal bead again to make another looped fringe. Repeat from * one more time to make a third loop.

Step 4: Pass through the 4 circle beads again, down through the focal bead, and then into one of the loops. Tie a small square knot, then pass through a few more loop beads to hide the thread tail. Pull the thread up and cut it close to the beads so the end pops back into the loop of beads. Repeat with the other thread tail.

Step 5: Open the ear wire's bottom loop and attach it to the 4-bead circle with needle-nose pliers. Close the loop, making sure there are no gaps.

Step 6: Repeat all steps for the second earring.

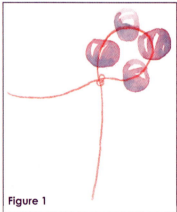

Figure 1

Figure 2